Lúcia Helena da Silva

Hannah Arendt's Question of Freedom in the Context of the American Revolution

Lúcia Helena da Silva

Hannah Arendt's Question of Freedom in the Context of the American Revolution

Without Freedom there is no Politics

ScienciaScripts

Imprint

Any brand names and product names mentioned in this book are subject to trademark, brand or patent protection and are trademarks or registered trademarks of their respective holders. The use of brand names, product names, common names, trade names, product descriptions etc. even without a particular marking in this work is in no way to be construed to mean that such names may be regarded as unrestricted in respect of trademark and brand protection legislation and could thus be used by anyone.

Cover image: www.ingimage.com

This book is a translation from the original published under ISBN 978-3-330-75539-0.

Publisher:
Sciencia Scripts
is a trademark of
Dodo Books Indian Ocean Ltd. and OmniScriptum S.R.L publishing group

120 High Road, East Finchley, London, N2 9ED, United Kingdom
Str. Armeneasca 28/1, office 1, Chisinau MD-2012, Republic of Moldova, Europe
Printed at: see last page
ISBN: 978-620-8-05456-4

SUMMARY

INTRODUCTION

The theme of freedom has been the object of study for many thinkers since antiquity. Each of them has imprinted his own perspective and placed his own understanding on it, in order to conceptualize it in a certain way.

For Arendt, there is no way to conceptualize and understand freedom without considering a question of innumerable logical impossibilities. To construct her definition of freedom, the author "starts from the contradictory principle between our conscience and our moral principles" (AREDNT, 2000, p. 209).

In his conception, the question of freedom is the last of the great questions of traditional metaphysics "such as being, nothingness, the soul, nature, time, eternity, etc." to become a subject of philosophical inquiry. - to become a subject of philosophical inquiry. And even when freedom appeared on the philosophical scene, it was through the Christian tradition, imposed first by Paul with his conversion to Christianity, and then by Augustine" (ARENDT, 2000, p. 191). However, according to Arendt, there is a strong tendency towards axiomatic hypotheses, in which laws are established in the context of practical, and in particular political, questions (p. 190).

Arendt asserts that the only field in which freedom has been recognized, not as a problem, but as a fact of everyday life, is the field of politics, declaring that "the raison d'être of politics is freedom, and its field of experience is action" (ARENDT, 2000, p.191). As man is endowed with the gift of action, for her, action and politics, among all the capacities and potentialities of human life, are the only things we could not even conceive of without at least admitting the existence of freedom. In this sense, it is up to man, having received the gift of action, to create possibilities in political matters, between deeds and words, in the realm of the public sphere, that establish a reality of freedom, which belongs to him by right.

The aim of this paper is to discuss the relationship between politics and freedom, as established today, using Arendt's ideas. To do this, it is essential to delve into Arendt's concept of freedom, in order to explain how it relates to politics.

In the first chapter of this work, we will briefly reflect on the question of freedom in Hannah Arendt. The starting point will be the question of inner freedom and the implications of this analysis for the field of politics in Arendt's conception. Next, we will analyze what freedom is for Arendt, demonstrably experienced between deeds and words, with ancient Greece as paradigm. Finally, we will discuss political freedom from an Arendtian perspective.

In the second chapter, we'll show how freedom became present in revolutions, and what forms helped to create a gulf between freedom and politics. In this sense, we will analyze how the social question became an obstacle to the establishment of freedom, particularly in the French Revolution. We will discuss freedom as the cause of revolutions and analyze the question of councils in Arendt's conception.

The third chapter consists of an understanding of the issue of districts in Thomas Jefferson's perception, followed by a brief assessment of the relationship between Liberty and the Constitution.

In the fourth chapter, we'll show how, following the dissolution of the Roman trinity (religion, tradition, authority), political authority became the last of the three elements to disappear. The loss of religious sanction led to a change in the conception of the earthly nature of the absolute. With this in mind, we will assess where Robespierre and the Founding Fathers of the American Revolution found the legitimization of authority in the political realm. We will evaluate Jefferson's analysis and Robespierre's attitude to the question of the absolute.

Finally, we turn to Montesquieu and his reading of the foundations of political structure in the West. We will show how his perception of legitimacy and political power is justified. The aim is to show how Montesquieu's perception is reflected in the question of legitimacy and political power.

1. THE ARENDTIAN CONCEPT OF FREEDOM

1.1 Inner freedom

To understand what freedom is, Arendt first leads us to understand the principle of causality, for, she argues, it is this that governs our everyday behavior (ARENDT, 2000 p. 188). Causality, according to Arendt, "constituted a category of mind for organizing sensory data, whatever their nature, thus making experience possible" (VE. 190).

We are well aware of the importance of this change of direction for philosophy. Philosophy must no longer concern itself with an explanatory claim about the world and things, with the various sciences explaining the world and its aspects accessible to our experience. By turning to the contents or phenomena existing in consciousness, we finally find an object that enables it to become an authentic science, as its founder Edmund Husserl (1859-1938) intended. But this content lends itself more to description than to measurement. It is clear, then, that this description is the function of this new philosophy (GALEFFI, 2000, p. 14).

After 1900, philosophy faced competition from the empirical sciences in the academic world. Philosophy professors at universities were trying to regain their leading role in the world of knowledge. In this context, Husserl wanted to consolidate philosophy's *status* as a fundamental science. Husserl even spoke of the precarious state of academic philosophy in his day. - In the journal *Logos* (I, 1911), he developed his program in the aforementioned article *"Philosophy as the science of rigor"*. Since phenomenology is not based on the data of experience or on the experience of realities, its task is to seek out the ideal possibilities of experience. The means to this end is intuition. This is why Husserl (1965) states:

But it is the very nature of philosophy, since it goes back to its extreme origins, to situate its scientific work in the spheres of direct intuition, and it is the greatest progress of our time to recognize that philosophical intuition in its authentic sense, the phenomenological perception of Being, opens up an immense field of work and leads to a science which, without all the indirectly symbolic and maternal methods, without the apparatus of conditions and proofs, does not fail to result in vast intellections of the most rigorous and decisive kind for all subsequent philosophy (p. 73). 73.

Reducing the importance of causality in knowledge reintroduces the discussion of freedom. According to Hannah Arendt, in practical matters we are free; in theoretical matters, we are subject to causality. However, when it comes to freedom in all practical fields, and especially in political ones, human freedom is a self-evident truth. And, she warns us, "on this axiomatic assumption, laws are established in human communities, decisions are made and judgments are pronounced" (ARENDT, 2000, p. 189).In *Between Past and Future,* Arendt (1961) describes how, in all areas of theoretical and scientific activity, we proceed on the contrary according to the no less self-evident truth of *nihi ex nihilo, nihil sine* causa, i.e. that "our very life is ultimately subject to causality" (p. 189) and that there may be a self in the world.

above all, free within ourselves. As freedom is a theme that runs through Hannah Arendt's entire work, it is the basis and foundation of her analyses of man's political condition, and of her critique of the inversion of values in modernity. It is therefore a highly relevant theme for understanding her thought, as well as for understanding the innovations promoted by the modern era.

Arendt's effort, in making freedom the center of her thought, was to stage the liberating condition of man who, at the beginning of the Christian era and throughout modernity, denied the external character of freedom, transposing it into the space of interiority, of consciousness, to which no one has access. According to the author, the invention of freedom is part of human history. It was in Greek antiquity, "[...] when men began to live a politically organized life, that it imposed itself on the human scene as an aprioristic value in relations between them" (SOUZA, 2008, p. 113).

Arendt's work is full of considerations about ancient Greece, and Socrates in particular. Although he left nothing written, it is to him that she turns in many of her works, praising the philosopher for the way he valued and participated in the *agora and gymnasiums of* the political sphere. Socrates is seen by Arendt as one of the thinkers who can perhaps best propose solutions to today's problems. The name Socrates appears quite frequently in Arendt's work, both in her writings of the 1950s and in her posthumous writings. Arendt returns to Socrates to study his relationship with politics and thought. She praises Socrates insofar as he values the public sphere and participates in the meetings of the *agora,* where he perceives men in the plural and lives *among them.* The idea of plurality appears constantly in Hannah Arendt's Socrates, particularly with regard to the idea of the Socratic two-in-one. On the other hand, Arendt questions Socratic morality and its "efficacy" in the face of politics (ECCEL, 2011, p. 3).

The two-in-one consists in being alone with oneself and dialoguing with one's inner self, as if, by disconnecting from the outside world, each of us were maintaining a dialogue with ourselves, in which one self responds to what the other asks of it. This is what she believes is most important, because when we dialogue with ourselves, there is plurality, i.e. man is not alone. The author states: "[...] experiences of inner freedom are derivative in the sense that they always presuppose a withdrawal from the world where freedom has been denied to an interiority to which no one else has access" (ARENDT, 2000, p. 192).

At another point in Arendt's reflection on the philosopher Socrates, she focuses much of her attention on several of his works: the question of plurality. Socrates, when he places man at the center of his thinking, is seen by her as the thinker who actually contributes to the resolution of many of humanity's current problems. The two-in-one does not subject man to the condition of isolation from the world, for it is already considered plural not to think alone. However, it is from here that man will formulate ideas, which will be associated with others. What's worth noting is that man never seems to be alone, and that things apparently happen in a way that doesn't "facilitate" solitude, but on the contrary, favors man's ever-plural nature. However, when it comes to politics, she disagrees with this point of Socrates' thinking, because for him, it's his conscience that's the most important thing, and that leads him to be at peace with himself. And this line of thought becomes dangerous in political thinking, because there's the possibility that the politician will act in the public sphere following his own conscience - in a singular space, where plurality doesn't occur, leaving room for arbitrary and dishonest actions. "By putting his conscience and his soul first, he thinks more of his soul than of the world" (ARENDT, 2000, p. 209). In this sense, Arendt (2005) is quite clear in her statement:

Living with others begins with living with oneself. It is in contact with others, then, that Arendtian thought [...] on Socrates offers various possibilities to help bring about ideas that will contribute greatly to transformations in everyday life (p. 207).

For Arendt, the freedom associated with politics is not a phenomenon of the will, for it is not a matter of choosing between a good thing and a bad thing, but of the common action of men. For the author, when each man, with his singularity, unites with other singular beings in political debates, they are truly free, for freedom is experienced and demonstrated in action. "And action, being free, is neither under the direction of the intellect, nor under the dictation of the will. Although it needs both to reach a certain goal, it derives from principles, and these do not come from within the self as motives do" (ARENDT, 2000, p. 209).

Inner freedom, from an Arendtian perspective, allows us to observe, at first, the difficulty raised by this question, given the contradiction between our conscience and our moral principles, of which the Christian-Augustinian tradition is *hvre-arbilrio*. While we are told that we are free, our everyday experience places us in conformity with the principle of causality, in which, according to Arendt (1961):

Our lives are ultimately subject to causality. The role that force plays in nature as the cause of movement and motive as the cause of behavior in the mental sphere are still hidden from observation, both from the inspection of our neighbors and from introspection. And this practical unpredictability is not a criterion of freedom; it means that we are not capable of knowing the causes that come into play (p. 55).

In her analyses of political issues, Arendt treats the problem of freedom as crucial, calling it the "obscure forest where philosophy has lost its way" (ARENDT, 2000): "The fact that has led to this obscurity is that the phenomenon of freedom does not arise in the sphere of thought, in a dialogue with itself. Philosophical tradition has deformed the very idea of freedom instead of clarifying it" (p. 191).

In the midst of so many ways of presenting freedom, be it through will or causality, we are allowed to turn to Kant, who saved freedom from this double assault. According to Hannah Arendt, by distinguishing between a theoretical or "pure" reason and a "practical reason", the center of which is the will. We realize that this solution, opposing the diktat of the will to the understanding of reason, is quite ingenious and may even suffice to establish a moral law whose logical coherence has nothing to envy that of natural law. For Arendt, it hardly eliminates the greatest and most dangerous difficulty, which is thought itself; in her theoretical and pre-theoretical forms (ARENDT, 2000), she says that:

To make freedom disappear without mentioning the fact that it must seem really strange "that the faculty of the will, whose essential activity consists in imposing and commanding, is the one that shelters freedom" (p.190).

For Hannah Arendt, the emergence of the problem of freedom in Augustine was preceded by a conscious attempt to dissociate the notion of freedom from politics, resulting in a formulation such that it was possible to be a slave in the world and still be free. This is partly due to the Christian concept of political freedom, which "arose from the mistrust and hostility of the early Christians towards the political sphere as such, from which they claimed exemption in order to be free" (ARENDT, 2000).

Of all the classical thinkers, it is in Augustine that freedom becomes a point of reference for Arendt. When reflecting on the question of freedom, she turns to Greek and Christian experience, and enters into a dialogue with both ways of conceiving freedom.

From this dialogue stems Arendt's perception that, although in Augustine freedom becomes an attribute of the mental faculties, i.e. the will, Arendt (2013) states:

Without the mental freedom to deny or affirm existence, to say yes or no, - not just to statements or to express agreement or disagreement, but to things as they present themselves, beyond agreement and disagreement, to our organs of perception and knowledge - no action would be possible, and action is exactly what politics is made of (p. 15).

Freedom was conceived as the last of the traditional metaphysical questions to be studied on the philosophical stage. Freedom was introduced by the Christian tradition after Paul's conversation, and then Augustine equated it with *free will*. In this way, inner freedom was emphasized, giving thought the quality of will. Since then, conscience and moral principles have occupied a central place in inner freedom and in the tradition of Western thought. It is understandable, from Arendt's perspective, that modern man, at the height of the question of singularity, placed inner freedom at the center of freedom of thought (ARENDT, 2000, p. 193). However, Arendt (2000) tells us: "Before Augustine, there had already been a conscious attempt to separate the notion of freedom from politics" (p. 194).

This is how inner freedom came to the fore, giving thought the quality of will. From then on, conscience and moral principles occupied a central place in the field of inner freedom and in the tradition of Western thought. It can be argued that man would not know inner freedom if he had not first experienced the condition of being free as a worldly, tangible reality. He has only become aware of freedom or its opposite in relation to others, and not in relation to himself.

However, she assures us that it would not be possible to understand inner freedom if freedom had not first historically been the way people lived. The phenomenon of free will would lead us to believe that freedom did not exist in antiquity, when "I want" and "I can" coincided. Arendt's (2000) analysis is worth highlighting here: "If freedom were really no longer a phenomenon of arbitration, we would be forced to conclude that the ancients did not know freedom" (p. 204).

In short, the concept of inner freedom, or freedom based on conscience, has become a benchmark for feeling free, and has extended throughout modernity, even if, at certain times, the concept of freedom has also been thought of in terms of political freedom. For Arendt, however, freedom is born of action. Man's exteriority to the world can only be expressed through action. From her conception of freedom, the author leads us to understand that "freedom" experienced in thought is an illusion when we think of a concrete, apparent world. Freedom becomes a reality if it is translated and perceived as a common action between men, through deeds and words.

1.2 Between words and deeds

"To exist as a human being is to reveal oneself through action and discourse.

(ARENDT, 1987, p. 189)

Arendt's writings show that it is part of the human condition to be able to reveal oneself through actions and words. For the author, human plurality is the basic condition for action and discourse between singular beings, but we realize that human beings are not always willing to reveal their latent *selves*. The author's approach to political freedom, not as a freedom of the will, but as the freedom on which classical antiquity is founded.

Arendt (1987) points out that the freedom to act and speak rests on man's ability to start something new. Forms of domination have tried to exterminate man's spontaneity. But the world is renewed every day by birth. The course of the world can be predicted if newborn babies are deprived of their spontaneity. For Arendt, it is in the nature of beginnings to start something new. For Arendt, there is something that cannot be predicted from everything that has gone before. "Unpredictability is inherent in every beginning" (p. 190).

With Hannah Arendt, we realize that human plurality is the basic condition of action and discourse, and that it has two aspects: it is equal and it is different. It is equal when people have equal conditions for understanding each other, for understanding their history and that of their ancestors, and for planning for the future and meeting the needs of future generations. It is different when we realize that "if each human being were no different from those who have existed or will exist, there would be no need to speak and act to make ourselves understood" (LAFER, 1987, p. 192).

For Arendt, being different is not the same as being other. In man, the otherness (characteristic circumstance or condition that develops through relations of difference and contrast) that he has in common with everything, and which he therefore shares with everything that exists. This distinction becomes singularity, because only man is capable of communicating himself. Human plurality thus becomes the paradoxical plurality of singular beings. As Lafer (1987) puts it:

In action and discourse, men show who they are, actively reveal their personal and singular identities, and thus present themselves to the human world, while their physical identities are revealed, without any activity of their own, in the singular conformation of the body and the singular sound of the voice (p. 192).

According to Arendt, there is a close relationship between action and discourse, for without discourse, action would cease to be itself. Action reveals itself humanly through words. The author of words announces: "[...] what he has done, what he is doing and what he intends to do. As such, it reveals the agent as well as the accomplished act" (LAFER, 1987, p. 192).

However, there is 1ашбёш a fear of revealing oneself among men. The individual then becomes solitary, because in contact with others he becomes clear who he is as a subject, and it's not uncommon to observe the human desire to hide what he is in silence or total passivity. "In human coexistence, the revealing quality of speech and action is brought to the fore, and there must be a human willingness to reveal one's individuality" (LAFER, 1987, p. 191).

For Arendt, action cannot exist in isolation. In other words, to be isolated is to be deprived of the capacity to act. Human relations and history show us that actions and discourses take place between people, and that their actions and words come from the fact that they have acted and spoken directly with one another. There are, however, different networks of relationships in which human stories are objectified. However, Lafer (1987) warns us: "Action and discourse almost always refer to a mediation, which varies from group to group, so that most words and deeds, while revealing the agent who speaks and acts, refer to a worldly, objective reality" (p. 183). The world is what stands between men, from which they derive their specific, objective, worldly interests. But these interests are, in the most literal sense of the word, something that *intersects,* that is between men and, therefore, connects and interconnects them. Referring to Dante, Lafer (1987) observes:

Indeed, in all action, the agent's main intention, whether acting out of natural necessity or his own will, is to reveal his own image. Thus, every agent, insofar as he acts, experiences pleasure in acting; since everything that exists desires its own existence, and since, in action, the agent's existence is in some way intensified, pleasure necessarily results. Thus, no one acts without manifesting (by acting) his latent self (p. 188).

We realize that Arendt helps us understand the human need to reveal ourselves. In this case, there is a pleasure in acting. However, there is not always a human desire to reveal oneself, but we can see that in various sectors, there are still men who are ready to unite and serve, whether in NGOs, religious, political or sporting movements, with a passion and an ideal for what they do, because this is how, according to the author, freedom manifests itself. The image of the human being is always revealed when, in word and deed, his very existence is intensified. In this sense, action is the manifestation of the latent self. The result of this revelation of his image is the main element that enables him to always want to act, because all this translates into the pleasure of acting.

Hannah Arendt's conception of freedom lies between actions and words. In her writings, we see how inherent in the human condition is the ability to express oneself beyond the organic. This capacity comes through speech and action. It is words that insert us into the world. But it is precisely language, the verb of action, to act, that indicates initiative. Thanks to it, we realize that something new is on the way. Acting means that man is expected to be unpredictable. Action needs discourse, because without it there would be no agent of discourse. In discourse and action, man shows himself as he is, for "it is in human coexistence - in plurality with other singular beings - that the manifestation of his latent *self* is possible" (LAFER, 1987, p. 191).

According to Arendt, plurality can exist and be present in any group to which one belongs. However, it is necessary to have the desire to reveal oneself, for it is in human coexistence that the revelatory quality of action and speech, in their inherent unpredictability, emerges. From this we can deduce that the only thing indispensable to the manifestation of freedom in the public sphere is coexistence between singular beings.

1.3 Political freedom

In proposing the theme of the question of political freedom, we must turn to Arendt's understanding of how it occurs in the political sphere, and how the word freedom has been associated over time by political actors, philosophers and Christians. According to Arendt, this perception has implications for how freedom has been treated in the context of political issues. She states: "The raison d'être of politics is freedom" (ARENDT, 2000, p. 192). For Hannah Arendt, to consider that the raison d'être of politics is freedom is also to realize that the complexity of the word freedom comes from the different influences on how freedom has been interpreted throughout history.

In the ancient Greek tradition, freedom was conceived as a demonstrable fact. It was the possibility of leaving one's home and debating with others on an equal footing. For Arendt, the *self with others* is the moment when demonstrable fact and politics coincide. This is a situation that differs from human relations, such as tribal or family relations, where the necessities of life take the place of freedom and eventually relegate it to the background. Action, freedom and politics, in the author's conception, are intertwined in the same sense. But when one of these elements is affected, the others suffer. Thus, freedom is conditioned by action. According to Arendt (1987): "Men are free only when they act, for to act and to be free are the same thing" (p. 15-20). Arendt asserts that the Greek *polis* was precisely the "form of government that offered men a space of appearance where they could act - a kind of amphitheater where freedom could appear" (p. 201).

According to the thinker, when men discuss in the public space, and at the same time each in his singularity (if they address the Greek *polis*), then, together, plurality prevails. Political issues were debated, freedom and dignity were exercised in the realm of politics, and at that point, action was the realm of experience. Action, for Hannah Arendt, is free when it demonstrates that it is capable of transcending the motives and objectives for which men act. The men of the Greek *polis* acted in common and needed the presence of other men; they depended on others for action to appear. Schio (2012) asserts: "Men are free - unlike the gift of freedom - while they act, neither before nor after; for being free and acting are one and the same thing" (p. 153). We can see that words and actions bring about changes in the way people act and think. And, at times, the human form of projection has very strong allies in terms of words and agendas to influence the way certain groups think and act, be they political, religious or professional. There's a lot of force in what's said, and the weight of the word is much greater when the language comes from people who play a role with an audience, and say they "represent" it politically, as if that possibility of representation actually existed, and make that audience, fallaciously, the target of their personal considerations. However, when groups of people exercise and act together, building relationships, debating the interests of the majority with different opinions, then freedom is present.

After experiences such as the rise of totalitarianism and the subordination of all spheres of life to the demands of politics and the consequent neglect of civil rights. Thus, political freedom in Arendtian terms is perceived as incompatible, since to be free, action must also be free.

The motives that lead to action cannot presuppose an intentional end as a foreseeable effect; in other words, action must be carried out without any pretense of domination and power. The Machiavellian concept of virtuosity in the context of political issues is the subject of discussion and research. "Virtuosity - the art of accomplishment - perfection in the very execution of the task, not in the final product." (SCHIO, 2012) asserts that:

Political action places man before opportunity, before fortune, unlike the artist who places his perfection in the act of realization. And his creative process is such that the final product is the most pleasing to the public. It is only at the end of the process that virtuosity is shown and appreciated by the public (SCHIO, p. 156).

The politician, as a man of action, has something in common with the artist as far as the world is concerned". However, in acting virtuously, the politician does not place his fulfillment in action. As an art, he plays a different role to that of the artist, for his claim is not to situate himself in relation to the relationships established with others. At times, there is no perfection either in the execution or in the final product of the action, which minimizes his creative process, abandoning himself to opportunities that may bring him benefits. These benefits generally play no role from the point of view of the audience, who place their expectations and hopes in the performance (SCHIO, 2012, p. 156).

The truth is, the perfection that artists strive for in the execution of their task should be the same as that which politicians strive for when it comes to citizens and how they relate to them. The artist practices his art to the best of his ability, but only until the end result can be appreciated by the public. The politician, on the other hand, must seek a close relationship with the population, who will be for him the indicator of the practices necessary to fulfill his role, and joint action will be the best way to exercise freedom in politics. Men must therefore leave the comfort of their homes and take a more active part in political life if freedom is to manifest itself.

Despite the author's perception of freedom's incompatibility with politics, we can't lose our starting point, and can always turn to the way the Greeks dealt with the question of freedom in the context of politics. And as we well know, despite all the negative influences that Christian tradition and sovereign power have tried to exert on mankind down the ages, it's up to man, with words and auguries, to be the protagonist of his own history.

2. REVOLUTION AND FREEDOM IN THE LIGHT OF HANNAH ARENDT

2.1 The quest for freedom as the cause of revolutions

We can turn to Hannah Arendt to understand how the question of freedom has been the target of revolutions. The author points out that "[...] what has determined the very existence of politics is the cause of freedom against tyranny" (ARENDT, 1990, p.9). Throughout history, the concept of freedom has often been forgotten.

For the author, the revolutionary phenomenon is what has most marked the physiognomy of the 20th century, unlike the 19th century, during which nationalism - internationalism, capitalism - imperialism, socialism - communism, though invoked, ended up losing touch with the world's main realities. Revolutions constitute the concept of freedom in their political questioning, surviving all ideological justifications, bringing with them the hope of human emancipation. This has led man, throughout history, to "assume, among the powers of the Earth, the just and independent position conferred upon him by the laws of Nature and the God of Nature" (ARENDT, 1990, p. 9).

Revolutions, in the truest sense of the word, did not exist before the modern era, and they have remained present in all the most important political statistics. Worse still: "the idea of freedom at the center of political debates takes on the dimension of discussions about war and the justified use of violence". War is rarely linked to the denial of freedom. The concept of freedom is thus buried (ARENDT, 1990, p. 10).

Justifications for wars and revolutions, even on a theoretical level, are quite old in the Greek *polis*, where the basis was persuasion, not violence. However, outside the walls of the polis, according to Thucydides: "The strong did what they could, while the weak suffered what was necessary" (ARENDT, 1990, p. 10).

According to Arendt, an obvious prerequisite would always be the conviction that political relations, in their normal course, do not fall into the realm of violence. The city, in the sense of the theoretical state, was defined as a way of life based exclusively on persuasion and not on violence. This is how the justifications for war emerged in Roman antiquity, along with the first idea that there were just and unjust wars, but that they were not about freedom. The realities of power politics demanded conquest and expansion to defend invested capital and the maintenance of power in the face of the emergence of new threatening powers, or to sustain a certain balance of power, seen as necessities, i.e. as legitimate reasons to justify the decision to resort to arms (ARENDT, 1990, p. 11).

The idea that aggression is a crime and that wars can only be justified if they are aimed at repelling or preventing aggression acquired practical or theoretical relevance after the First World War demonstrated the horrific destructive potential of war under the conditions of modern technology. We are, however, aware of the absence of the freedom argument in traditional justifications for war as the last refuge of international politics. In a second justification of war, what we see, according to the author, is:

That the days of governments are numbered, for since the First World War, no state or form of government has been strong enough to survive defeat in war: the days of all governments are numbered (ARENDT, 1990, p. 11).

The third justification for war shows us a radical change in nature, with the armed forces unable to defend the civilian population. From the First World War onwards, intimidation is used more to avoid war than to win it (ARENDT, 1990, p. 13). We can introduce here an important notion in Arendt, the interrelation between war and revolution, which for her is an ancient phenomenon, as are revolutions that were preceded and accompanied by a war of liberation, as was the American Revolution. And which led to wars of defense and aggression, as was the case with the French Revolution. Admitting that the end of the war was a revolution became natural, as did assuming that the justification was the revolutionary cause of freedom. This is how the twentieth century, characterized by wars and revolutions, took shape. The politics of force became an obsolete and useless profession for those who believed in it. And this despite the close relationship between war and revolution. "Twenty years later, it has become almost natural that the end of war is revolution, and that the only cause that can justify it is the revolutionary cause of freedom" (ARENDT, 1990, p. 14).

However, we do see Arendt turn her gaze to the totalitarian regime, because for her the two pillars that support it are ideology and terror, and they articulate in a complementary way: where the regime's supposed enemies are massacred. "It is because of this silence that violence is a marginal phenomenon in the political field; because man, insofar as he is a political being, is endowed with the power of speech, and because of this absence of speech, political theory has almost nothing to say about the phenomenon of violence" (ARENDT, 1990, p. 15).

The atrocities committed by the Nazis in the extermination camps finally led Arendt (1951) to the problems that, from then on, would occupy the center of her thought when it became clear that violence was becoming the center of politics. And her pain is even greater when we see that the totalitarian regime has thrown down all the old political theories in unprecedented barbarity, showing the tragic face of politics and the progressive destruction of the public sphere. In this context, the notion of plurality, agendas and words were banished from the public sphere. What's more, totalitarianism deprives man of his ability to think, from which evil has taken on an ethico-political perspective (p. 527).

The search for freedom as the cause of revolutions is evident in Arendt's observation: "Man is free when he acts and speaks, which always allows something new to begin. In this context, there is no room for any form of domination that would tend to exterminate his spontaneity. Nevertheless, Hannah Arendt has distinguished herself by her sensitivity to the crisis of values, the dissolution of public spaces, the domestication of the masses by the wiles of capital and consumerist illusions, the destruction of political culture and the cult of public and common values, anti-Semitic persecutions and the castration of freedom (ARENDT, 1951, p. 372).

The French revolutionary phenomenon is linked to the social question and its dehumanizing nature, imposing the social question in an overwhelming and immediate way. "The course of the French Revolution was diverted from its primitive course almost from the start by the urgency of suffering; this was provoked by the demands of liberation, not from tyranny, but from necessity, and driven by the unlimited proportions of the people's misery and the pity that this misery inspired. This is why revolutionaries were preoccupied with the social question, in which men deprived of the basic elements of survival have their biological conditions affected" (ARENDT, 1990, p. 73).

Finally, what most caught Hannah Arendt's attention regarding freedom as the cause of revolutions was what happened during the North American Revolution, in which spontaneous groups emerged from the thirteen colonies in search of independence and the establishment of political freedom, when there was no tension between political and biological necessity.

2.2 Social issues: an obstacle to the establishment of freedom by the French Revolution

For Hannah Arendt, the early twentieth century is strongly marked by the category of revolutionary thought. The notion of historical necessity, assumed by the French Revolution, appears to be associated with the social question in an overwhelming and immediate way.

It is in the social sphere that Arendt defends and bases her critique of the way in which modern politics has developed. Parallel to the rise of the social sphere, we are witnessing the decline of the public sphere. In the 18th century, the existence of poverty "placed men under the dictates of absolute necessity". It was under the empire of this necessity that the crowd rushed to the aid of the French Revolution, inspired it and ruined it, because it was the crowd of the poor" (ARENDT, 1990, p. 59).

The concept of humanity has both ontological and political dimensions. Ontologically, in the sense that belonging to humanity guarantees the individual the possibility of carrying within him or herself the right to have rights. Politically, in the sense that the right to have rights will require international protection recognized in a perspective of humanity (LAFER, 2003, p. 114).

Arendt's political philosophy proposal for the reconstruction of human rights "is based on the recognition of the right to have rights". She sees Kantian universalist and cosmopolitan morality as the foundation for the construction of an international public space, in which politics and law are realized beyond the borders of national states (BRITO, 2013, p. 3).

The historical journey of human rights encountered many obstacles from its earliest years, just after the two great bourgeois revolutions. Arendt's contribution to its analysis was decisive, "in that she developed a theoretical path that enabled us to understand its true significance for philosophy and politics" (BRITO, 2013, p. 4).

Eighteenth-century France was experiencing severe economic difficulties, which particularly affected the Third Estate. Louis XVI's ministers' solution to the crisis was to raise taxes, which led to an innovation: the nobles and clergy, the ruling class who had hitherto been exempt from taxation, were included in the distribution, much to their dismay. The Third Estate comprised urban workers, peasants and the petty bourgeoisie. Taxes were paid only by this social stratum, in order to maintain the luxury of the nobility. As the lives of workers and peasants were extremely miserable, they wanted to improve their quality of life and work. The bourgeoisie, although enjoying a more important social position, wanted to participate in political life while enjoying greater economic freedom in their work. The political situation became tense and, under pressure from the king, he convened a National Constituent Assembly with the participation of the Estates-General. The council model consisted of representation from the three states that made up society, and each was entitled to one vote, which was already lost on the Third Estate, since the score would be two to one for the nobles and clergy, who were combined for the vote (HOBSBAWN, 1996, p. 18).

Then, tired of having no say in the matter, the Third Estate revolted and proclaimed itself the National Constituent Assembly, drafting a new constitution for France. The National Constituent Assembly passed laws abolishing the feudal and seigneurial systems, as well as tithing. Other laws prohibited the sale of public offices and tax exemptions for the privileged (HOBSBAWN, 1996, p. 14-15).

Little by little, the population has been plunged into a sea of protests. People took to the streets in search of food and weapons. Chaos began to grip Paris. Royal power became unbearable and unsustainable. The population no longer agreed with the situation. "There is no doubt that social inequality is one of the main reasons for the popular revolt" (HOBSBAWN, 1996, p. 19).

In the face of Parisian chaos, Arendt tells us that the social question came to be understood as the search for freedom from biological needs. Even the French revolutionaries began to concern themselves with the social question, because when men are deprived of the basic elements for survival, their biological conditions are affected (ARENDT, 1990, p. 73).

The original and most legitimate source of political power is man's desire to emancipate himself from the necessity of life. "It was only the emergence of technology, and not the emergence of modern political ideas as such, that came to disprove the old and terrible truth that only violence and domination over others could bring freedom to some men". The result was that necessity invaded the political sphere, the only sphere in which men can be truly free (ARENDT, 1990, p. 90).

Today, political debate has no place in people's daily lives, and the long-awaited political freedom does not exist. Arendt believed in the possibility of its realization. It hasn't materialized. What does exist is a biopolitics to maintain the body, and a mad rush in pursuit of exaggerated consumerism. Yet it is in the public space that people would be, in Arendt's conception, politically free. This leads us to think that we are not free, because political freedom in the sense of this reflection is not perceived today.

2.3 The question of advice in Hannah Arendt's political thought

The end of the revolution, contrary to Hannah Arendt's expectations when she took the example of ancient Greece and the legacy of the American Revolution, was a participatory politics in which freedom in politics could be exercised by men acting together. But what we see is, on the one hand, a revolutionary force claiming the right to make freedom a reality in the public sphere, and, on the other, a revolution that either ends in the disaster of terror, or ends in the establishment of a republic.

The men of the American Revolution decided and declared the independence of the United States. At this moment in history, freedom appeared in a demonstrable form in the public arena. LEON (2014) in his book - *Authority and Power,* states:

It is inherent in the very nature of human society that human beings turn to the knowledge and experience of others, in whom they place their trust because they attribute the right knowledge to them. This is rooted in an authentic conception of authority (p. 137).

The North American Revolution was to be the compass by which society would seek to orient itself, keeping alive the spirit of the revolutionaries. Yet the French Revolution, with its disastrous course due to the large number of people made destitute by biological necessity, runs counter to everything that was built in America.

From the French Revolution onwards, the pursuit of public happiness became the sole objective of councils. At this point in history, there are tensions between councils and parties, as their objectives differ. Claiming that the councils held to the same revolutionary ideals became utopian, as they didn't understand that, in the republic, party programs distanced them from their main objective, which had always been participation in the public sphere. "Action came to be interpreted in terms of the liberation and violence that preceded the American Declaration of Independence" (ARENDT, 1990, p. 101).

Thomas Jefferson realized, albeit belatedly, the danger of extinguishing the revolutionary force in the public sphere. He considered it a mortal danger to the republic that the people should have their place in the private sphere, for the government of the republic would no longer have room for those who had built it. Despite the measures he took to ensure that future generations would have the right to choose their own representatives. Later, he turned his attention to the drafting of the Constitution and, according to Arendt, realized the seemingly inevitable flaw in the structure of the republic, making the "Constitution perfect and immutable, as well as the risk of dissolving the public space for political questions" (ARENDT, 1990, p. 187).

During revolutions, councils eventually lose their place. The author quotes Benjamin Rush, in his book *DaRevolugao* (1990), on the dangerous new doctrine according to which: "all power emanates from the people, holding it only on election days. After that, it becomes the property of the rulers" (p. 186). Representation in modern politics succinctly confirms this quote, as the representative model as an alternative form of government after the establishment of the republic, where rulers and ruled were abolished, led to the disappearance of the revolutionary in the public sphere. The Grand Conseil Municipal of the Paris Commune was this communal council system, not the assemblies of voters that spread throughout France in the form of revolutionary societies. Arendt (1990) states: "Only the representatives of the people, not the people themselves, had the possibility of engaging in the activities of 'expression, discussion and decision', which, in a positive sense, are the activities of freedom" (p. 188).

The few rights that politics, particularly in Brazil, offers citizens are often not used properly. A transparency portal has been created where citizens have the right to follow the political life of their representatives. However, we hardly ever access it, and when we do, we don't pay for it. We end up not debating politics anywhere, convinced that nothing will change. Yet the demonstrations that took place across the country in late autumn 2013 tell us that it's time to change our conception of where the country's political life can go. This is a crisis that can bring something new, as Arendt (1951) tells us: "The fact remains that the crisis of our age and its main experience have given birth to an entirely new form of government which, as an ever-present potentiality and risk, unfortunately tends henceforth to remain with us [...]" (p. 445).

And how, today, there are many obstacles to establishing freedom in politics. The modern world does not allow us to think of devoting our time to the exercise of citizenship in the public sphere, because the demands of modernity are in contradiction with what was exercised in ancient Greece, as well as in the American Revolution, when men, in deed and word, exercised political freedom in common action. Today, the vital needs that prevent us from establishing freedom in the public sphere are compounded by our contempt for the fundamental issues of a citizen's life: health, education and the right to have a right.

"What the American Revolution effectively did was to bring the new experience and conception of power into the public domain. This has contributed to the inertia that prevents us from acting to establish freedom in politics. Now is the time - a change of attitude can help abolish the implications of social issues. With effective participation, we can contribute to a new way of doing politics. And may social issues never be an obstacle to establishing freedom in politics in a demonstrable way, thus giving new directions to the life of the citizen in society (ARENDT, 1990, p. 133).

"After the French Revolution, a new figure appeared in politics: the professional revolutionary. He presents himself in the exercise of power within the council, in a structured and scientific way, in total divergence with the revolutionary way that existed until then. He is totally different from the revolutionary who emerged spontaneously in the councils, willing to debate, to unite, with availability and courage where there were no leaders, but a great desire for freedom (ARENDT, 1990, p. 206).

The revolutionaries, once the revolution was over, thought that the revolutionary spirit was guaranteed to remain. They really were revolutionaries. But because they believed the revolutionary spirit would remain, they did nothing to preserve it. The founding of a new body politic and all the efforts to keep the constitutions "sacred" left them, after the revolution was over, unnoticed by the whole process. Robespierre called the institutions "pillars of democracy", because "a great number of men would replace them" at some point. However, he knew that the people, who organized themselves outside the National Assembly in their own political societies, would only inform their representatives that "the republic was to provide individuals with the means of subsistence, while the task of the legislators was to banish misery from mankind" (ARENDT, 1990, p. 194).

In his book *Da Revolugao* (1990), the author mentions the spontaneity with which councils came into being. There were professional revolutionary groups who, in the twentieth century, organized themselves in a structured way, seeking to prepare and execute with well-planned scientific precision. Councils were the space of freedom (ARENDT, 1990) "A represented people is not free, because the will cannot be represented" (p. 193).

The power the people believe they hold on election day *is* not guaranteed after the election. This power becomes the property of those in power. Through representation, the public interest is decided by the personal interest that resides in the vote. For Arendt, councils are spaces of freedom. In turn, this becomes the strength of councils, with greater representation in political decisions, in other words, a way of combating interests that do not benefit the people.

Despite their historic importance, councils still face resistance from the population, the vast majority of whom remain alienated from this form of politics. Some people work in the health and education sectors, for example, until they retire, without ever having attended a class council meeting. According to Arendt, the best way to demonstrate freedom in the public sphere is to involve the people in political decisions, to identify ways in which ordinary people can seek, or not seek, to strengthen councils, and to get them to find a way to meet all challenges and not let this spontaneous revolutionary form be banished. The strengthening of councils will be presented as an ancient form of struggle, so that the will of the people remains active and constant as in the history of social struggles. People's action in councils is decisive if, through the determination and commitment of the citizen to the struggle, there is to be an effective and real contribution, if freedom in the public sphere is to be affirmed in spontaneous organization in councils.

In short, people lost interest in the public sphere, because popular societies were totally incompatible with representative government. This tension between parties and councils led to the dissolution of freedom in the public sphere. However, as human action is, according to Arendt, always ready for a new beginning, popular participation in the public sphere is still possible in modern society.

3. THE CONSTITUTION OF FREEDOM IN HANNAH ARENDT'S CONCEPTION

3.1 District freedoms according to Jefferson

For Jefferson, according to Arendt (1968, p. 186), could constitutions be immutable? How and from what point of view did he evaluate action? What did he think of the district system, and what role did it play in relation to councils and the replacement of direct popular action by representation? To better understand our reflections on Jefferson's understanding of district liberty, we'll begin by analyzing who Thomas Jefferson was.

Thomas Jefferson - author of the Declaration of Independence and the Virginia Statute for Religious Freedom, third President of the United States and founder of the University of Virginia - expressed the aspirations of a new America like no other individual of his time. As public servant, historian, philosopher and farm owner, he served his country for more than five decades (MALONE, 1993).

After attending the College of William and Mary, Jefferson practiced law and served in local government as a magistrate, lieutenant-counselor and member of the House of Burgesses during his working life. As a member of the Continental Congress, he was chosen in 1776 to draft the Declaration of Independence, since considered a charter of American and universal liberties. This document proclaims that all men are equal in rights, regardless of birth, wealth or *status,* and that government is the servant, not the master, of the people.

Jefferson left Congress in 1776. He returned to Virginia and served in the legislature. Elected governor between 1779 and 1781, he was the subject of an inquiry into his conduct during the last year of his term, an inquiry which, although ultimately totally dismissed, would leave him *stinging in* the face of criticism for the rest of his life (MALONE, 1993).

During the brief period of his life following his administration, Jefferson wrote *Notes on the State of Virginia.* In 1784, he again entered public service, in France, first as commissioner of commerce, then as Benjamin Franklin's successor as minister. During this period, he avidly studied European culture (MALONE, 1993).

In 1790, Jefferson accepted the post of Secretary of State under his friend George Washington. His tenure was marked by opposition to Alexander Hamilton's pro-British policies. In 1796, as the Republican candidate for President, he became Vice-President after losing to John Adams by three electoral votes (htt://WWW.site/Jefferson/Tomaz-jefferson-brief-biografy).

Four years later, Jefferson defeated Adams to become president. It was the first peaceful transfer of authority from one party to another in the history of the young nation. The purchase of the Louisiana Territory in 1803 and his support for the Lewis and Clark expedition are perhaps the most notable achievements of his first term. During his second term, he encountered more difficulties, both at home and abroad. He is best remembered for his efforts to maintain neutrality in the midst of the conflict between Britain and France, as his efforts failed to prevent war with Britain in 1812 (htt://WWW.site/Jefferson/Tomaz-jefferson-brief-biografy).

In 1809, his friend James Madison succeeded him as president, and he remained at Monticello for the next 17 years of his life. During this period, he sold his collection of books to form the nucleus of the Library of Congress. At the age of 76, Jefferson embarked on his last great public service: founding the University of Virginia. He led the legislative campaign for its charter, secured its location, designed its buildings and served as its first rector. Thomas Jefferson died on July 4, 1826 (htt://WW.site/Jefferson/Tomaz-jefferson-brief-biografy).

The British colonized the Atlantic coast region of the United States, where thirteen colonies were founded. These colonies, initially very different and far apart politically and culturally, united and declared their independence. This independence was recognized by the United Kingdom after the end of the American Revolution of 1776, in 1783, under the terms of the Treaty of Paris. The thirteen colonies took this step because the British were taking advantage of North America by levying taxes to pay for the losses of British-led wars. The thirteen colonies therefore decided to be independent and waged war against the metropolis, with the support of France and Spain. The result was the United States, the first to adopt a presidential republic (htt://WWW.site/Jefferson/Tomaz-jefferson-brief- biografy).

What was beginning to worry Jefferson was that this republic, which had been established by the force of revolutionaries and according to the men of the revolution, was "[...] the only form of government that is eternally at war, frankly or secretly, with the rights of man". However, the form this republic took, according to Arendt, left no space in this system of government reserved for the exercise of the qualities with which it had been constructed. This was the price the revolutionaries had to pay for founding it.

For Arendt, Jefferson realized more clearly and demonstrated more passionately than anyone else the inevitable flaw in the structure of the republic on the American stage. How could he make the Constitution immutable, make it so sacred that it could not be touched? So he "concluded": "Nothing is immutable, except the inalienable and inherent rights of man" (ARENDT, 1990, p. 186). Among these rights, he included the right to revolution and rebellion.

The revolutionary spirit and the action of the men of the revolution, before the advent of the French Revolution, were strongly defended by Jefferson. However, what guided the debates on the problem of action in the revolutionary spirit was obscured. Hence the author's assertion that it was all wrong. But the French Revolution was catastrophic and, from then on, action was viewed from the angle of destruction, which eventually led him to change his position, given the new lessons learned, where the space for freedom was annihilated (ARENDT, 1990). To regard the founding of the republic as an achieved goal, leaving the revolutionary force useless from that point on, would be to condemn his own failure. What for Jefferson meant a seemingly inevitable flaw in the structure of the republic on the American political scene, making the constitution immutable was the "most ridiculous and insolent of all tyrannies" (p. 187).

Jefferson proposed the Declaration of Independence and then turned his attention to drafting the Constitution and establishing an entirely new government. In this proposal, a new form and different instruments for the Constitution emerged, among them: A revision of the Constitution in pre-established periods, which would include successive generations, admitting that each generation has "the right to choose for itself the form of government" it deems appropriate to promote its own happiness. But what we see is a way of making future generations choose their own representatives. Action is wrongly confused with liberation (ARENDT, 1990, p. 195).

With political freedom frustrated, Jefferson proposed periodic reforms of the constitution from generation to generation, on the grounds that each generation had "the right to choose its own form of government". For Arendt, this was a somewhat unexpected way of ensuring that each generation had the "right to appoint its representatives to conventions". She wanted to guarantee the whole process that took place during the Revolution. The result was that representation became a substitute for direct popular action. Republics came to be defined as representative governments, thus distinguishing themselves from democracies. Representatives became elected "representatives". ARENDT (1990) states that:

"The result of this form of government was that the people were not admitted into the public sphere, which became the task of government, thus becoming the privilege of the few, where

Jefferson called men's political talents 'virtuous aptitudes'" (P. 191).

This new form of representative government ends up making people forget everything they experienced in ancient Greece, as well as in the American Revolution in joint action. The feeling of being merely represented makes them apathetic and demotivated, and it's only a short step from there to the dissolution of the public sphere. In the Paris Communes, famous for their 48 secessions, there was originally no popular organization. Popular societies were incompatible with representative government. Robespierre, who nevertheless described them as "pillars of democracy", emphatically opposed them when he took power. Shortly afterwards, Saint-Jus did the same. And, with the district system, the Paris Commune was discarded at the end of the Revolution (ARENDT, 1990, p. 195).

A new figure appeared on the political scene after the French Revolution: the professional revolutionary, who, unlike the one who emerged from among the people with a joint action between deeds and words, acted in a planned and precise way, totally different from the way revolution had been experienced until then. There was a decline in the public sphere, because the presence of these professionals made action in the public sphere unfeasible, because the interests were not the same and clash was inevitable, because spontaneity gave way to a totally new type, a model that added nothing to all that had already been experienced in the public sphere.

New mechanisms were used in representative government to gauge the people's reception of the new form of government, with the "Subdivision of the country into Districts", in order to generate smaller republics for "popular participation" (ARENDT, 1990, p. 206).For Jefferson, it was considered a danger that the people would participate in public power without being involved in the public sphere. However, Councils became the new form of government, destined to become superfluous, for where there is a divorce between knowledge and action, the space for freedom ceases to exist. And Jefferson ends up with a belated reflection on the district system. He says:

Elementary district republics, municipal republics, state republics and the Union republic will form a gradation of authorities, each backed by law, holding its full share of delegated power and truly constituting a system of checks and balances fundamental to government (ARENDT, 1990, p. 199).

Arendt notes that Jefferson remained silent when it came to defining elementary republics. According to the author, he sometimes mentioned, while listening to a proposal he had authored, that one of the advantages of the divisions he was proposing would be an excellent means of gathering the voice of the people in favor of representative government. But what he was really convinced of was that "let us set them in motion, if only for a purpose, and it will soon become evident that other purposes are also instruments" (ARENDT, 1990, p. 203).

In short, according to Arendt, Thomas Jefferson's aims were imprecise. However, she points out that even if he came to the conclusion that the dissolution of the public sphere would pose a constant danger to the consolidation of what had occurred so spontaneously in the American Revolution, the new form of government, with all the changes that had taken place and those that would take place, had to be able to ensure the security of the citizens. Later, reflecting on the Revolution, the new form of government, with all the changes that had taken place and those that would take place, would have to ensure the Constitution of Liberty. Starting by providing the public space with the right to liberty for the people, where they would have the opportunity to be happy, to share public happiness and public power (ARENDT, 1990, p. 204). Since then, the United States has gradually transformed itself into a superpower, exerting increasing political, economic, military and cultural influence on the world stage. The author has always linked the ideal of freedom to the experience of the North American revolution. Today, however, we are witnessing a total paradox: Americans are still afraid of terrorist attacks, in a mixture of fear and hatred, far from being a country that fights for freedom in the public sphere as it has done in the past.

3.2 Freedom and the Constitution

According to Arendt, revolutions - and even the American Revolution - were unable to ensure the establishment of the political freedom born in ancient Greece, and ended up creating a new form of "constitutional" government, resulting in a dose of civil rights in the form of a monarchy or republic, which ultimately merited only the appellation of limited government. For the author, Constitutions, contrary to popular belief, were not the result of revolutions - they somehow ended up being imposed after the failure of revolutions, which was seen as a sign of defeat rather than victory (ARENDT, 1990, p. 117).

In line with Arendt's argument, France and America needed constituent assemblies and special conventions, whose sole task was to draft a constitution. It was permissible to take the draft home and discuss it point by point before the people. If the articles of the Constitution were debated in state conventions, it would be popular participation that would give the government a Constitution in which the people constituted their own government, not the other way around (ARENDT, 1990, p. 116).

Another fundamental element that the revolutionaries failed to grasp was, on the one hand, the importance of founding a republic and, on the other, the fact that the real content of the Constitution was not the safeguarding of civil rights at all, but the establishment of an entirely new system of authority. What the regional charters and the loyal attachment of the colonies to the King and Parliament of England did for the people of America was to give them additional power and weight of authority. This colonial body politic of the New World became the foundation, not of power, but of authority (ARENDT, 1990, p. 118).

For Hannah Arendt (1990): "Power and authority differ as much as power and violence" (p. 118). The author points out that the monumental theme of Montesquieu's work was in fact the constitution of political liberty. But in this context, the word *constitution* lost all negative connotations, of limiting or negating power. The word now means: "The great temple of federal liberty" must be centered on the foundation and proper distribution of power. In this sense, *power and freedom* became linked, along with the *power of* representation (ARENDT, 1990, p. 120). It was impossible to believe that revolutionary power would still resist and remain intact in the face of the uncontrolled consolidation of the way in which the nature of power came to be exercised in political matters. Arendt (1990) states:

Power can only be contained, while remaining intact, by power, so that the principle of the separation of powers not only provides a guarantee against the monopolization of power by one part of government, but also offers a kind of mechanism, rooted in the very heart of government, by which new power is constantly generated, without, however, expanding at the expense of other centers or sources of power (p. 121).

An intriguing new problem has appeared on the scene: secularization. Christianity, which had hitherto dominated minds and hearts with its Roman power, rules and norms, was imposing its own ways of managing political, social and religious life. What would the establishment of a new authority look like without the domination of the Roman Empire? What would the new absolute be: a monarch, as in the French Revolution, or would it be more interesting to base power on the people, as in the American Revolution? According to Arendt, the problem of the absolute is inherent in the revolutionary event itself. Thus, the American revolutionaries offered us the chance of a perception, far from the historical conviction of what happened in the various revolutions where the authority of the monarch made us believe in its necessity (ARENDT, 1990, p. 156).

For Hannah Arendt, the American Revolution shows us an unforgettable example and teaches us an unprecedented bond, for this Revolution did not simply break out, but was led by men who resolved together, and were united in deed and word by the force of mutual commitments. This is what the author calls the "lost treasure" of the American Revolution: the forgotten popular participation and revolutionary spirit that led to American independence. All political affairs are and always have been dealt with within a framework of lakes and obligations for the future, such as laws and constitutions, treaties and alliances, all deriving, in the final analysis, from the ability to promote and maintain promise in the face of the intrinsic uncertainties of the future (ARENDT, 1990, p. 212).

iFinally, in the modern Constitution, the so-called democracy of the moderns has produced a new way of conceiving freedom. If, in ancient Greece and the American Revolution, freedom was conceived in terms of participation in the public sphere, where freedom could be demonstrably experienced, particularly in political matters, and where the citizen had the power to exercise his citizenship, in modern democracy freedom is understood as the exercise of civil rights and individual autonomy in the private sphere, the right to choose, the right to privacy, the right not to be imprisoned or tortured.

Liberty was seen by the ancients as something linked to the public sphere, whereas in modern times, it is clearly perceived that the concept of freedom is closely linked to the private sphere. However, to paraphrase Thomas Paine: "When a people constitutes a government, it must never renounce this conquest by letting a constitution be the act of government" (ARENDT, 1990, p. 116).

4. CONSIDERATIONS ON AUTHORITY AND LEGITIMACY IN HANNAH ARENDT'S THOUGHT

4.1 Jefferson's analysis

The motivation for the approach that follows is simple and straightforward: authority and legitimacy are relevant notions to analyze over time, and they remain relevant today because, while citizens' lifestyles have changed a great deal, the way in which they exercise politics has, as far as we can tell, changed little over time. In the following lines, we will analyze one of the founding fathers of the American Revolution.

Thomas Jefferson proposed the Declaration of Independence and then set about drafting the Constitution and establishing an entirely new government. This proposal gave birth to a new form and different instruments for the Constitution. Constitution-writing became a favorite pastime of the Founding Fathers, and Jefferson was no exception. However, the very notion of a Constitution eventually disintegrated and gradually lost its meaning. Indeed, the difference between a constitution, which is an act of government, and the constitution by which the people constitute a government is obvious. But in the New World, what has become very clear is that "man, by his very nature, is not qualified to be the holder of unlimited power". For rulers, it is always necessary to curb man and his thirst for power (ARENDT, 1990, p.117).

The revolutions of the seventeenth and eighteenth centuries, according to Arendt, were signs of a new spirit, the spirit of the modern age, but were to be no more than restorations. And the American Revolution was officially interpreted as a "restoration". or more precisely "freedom restored by God's blessings", as engraved on the large 1951 coat of arms (ARENDT, 1990, p.35).

For Jefferson, it was dangerous for the people to participate in public power without being part of the public sphere. However, Councils became the new form of government, destined to become superfluous, for where there is a divorce between knowledge and action, the space for freedom ceases to exist. For Arendt (1990), Jefferson makes a late reflection on the district system, saying that:

Elementary district republics, municipal republics, state republics and the Union republic will form a gradation of authorities, each supported by law, holding its full share of delegated power and truly constituting a system of checks and balances that is fundamental to government (p. 199).

Arendt notes that Jefferson remained silent when it came to defining elementary republics. According to the author, he sometimes mentioned, when listening to one of his proposals, as one of the advantages of the divisions he was proposing, that they were an excellent means of gathering the voice of the people in favor of representative government. But what he was really convinced of was that: "Let us begin them, if only for one purpose, and it will soon appear that other purposes are also instruments" (ARENDT, 1990, p. 203).

According to Arendt, Thomas Jefferson's objectives were imprecise. She points out that Thomas Jefferson may have concluded that the dissolution of the public sphere would constitute a constant danger to the consolidation of what had occurred so spontaneously in the American Revolution, and then reflect on the Revolution. This was the new form of government, with all the changes that had taken place, and the one that was supposed to guarantee the Constitution of liberty. Starting with ensuring that the public space guarantees the right to liberty for the people, where they have the opportunity to be happy, to share public happiness and public power (ARENDT, 1990, p. 204). In this sense, action depends on the will of men; a new absolute was not needed in the American Revolution, where human plurality was the decisive indicator. When there is unity and a common effort to achieve political action, it is men who legitimize laws.

What began to worry Jefferson was that this republic, which had been established by the force of revolutionaries and according to the men of the revolution, was "[...] the only form of government that is eternally at war, frankly or secretly, with the rights of man". In the form this republic took, according to Arendt, there was no space in this system of government reserved for the exercise of the qualities with which it had been constructed. This was the price the revolutionaries had to pay for founding it (ARENDT, 1990, p. 101).

The "Declaration of Independence refers to the 'pursuit of happiness' and not to the pursuit of public happiness". There is a loss of memory here, and Jefferson himself failed to notice the vagueness of this distinction, nor was it even noted in the Assembly debates (ARENDT, 1990, p.102).

When the subject of public happiness is broached directly, Jefferson and Adams begin jokingly discussing the possibilities of life after death. Behind the irony, we have the candid recognition that life in Congress, the joys of speeches, legislative activity, business arrangements, persuading and being persuaded, represented for Jefferson the same foretaste of eternal bliss as, for the medieval devotee, the delights of contemplation (ARENDT, 1990, p.105).

The American Revolution faced the most uncomfortable of all the problems of revolutionary government: the problem of the absolute. This problem cannot fail to appear in any revolution, for it is inherent in every revolutionary event, and we might never have become aware of it had the American Revolution not taken place. On the other hand, we are tempted to blame absolutism, which preceded all other revolutions (ARENDT, 1990, p.126).

Secularization, i.e. the emancipation of secular power from the authority of the Church. Absolute monarchy, which is generally rightly considered to have anticipated the nation-state, was also at the origin of the rise of the secular state, with its own dignity and splendor. The modern age began to encounter difficulties in the field of politics, which had been masked by the practice of absolutism for centuries and needed a new, fully satisfactory substitute to compensate for the loss of the religious sanction of authority in the person of the king, or rather in the institution of kingship (ARENDT, 1990, p.127).

For Arendt, there were several ways of interpreting what happened historically with the emergence of the turbulent problem of the absolute. But it was inevitable, because political organs and institutions had the absolute as inherent in traditional conceptions of law, and a deity eventually became necessary (ARENDT, 1990, p.157).

The laws themselves were seen as commandments interpreted in accordance with the voice of God who commanded men: "Thou shalt not do this". Clearly, such commandments could not be imposed without a higher religious sanction. To give authority and validity to human laws, it would be necessary to add to the "law of nature", as Jefferson did, the "God of nature", so that it mattered little whether, following the trend of the times, this god addressed his creatures by the voice of conscience or enlightened them with the light of reason, without appealing to biblical revelation. At a certain point in American history, when the transcendent source of authority for the laws of the new body politic followed the deistic beliefs of the founding fathers, Jefferson's famous words resonated: "We believe these truths to be self-evident." (ARENDT, 1990, p.156).

What was hoped for was that Jefferson, who at one time realized as no one else the danger of banning the public sphere, would now attest that: These truths are unprovable, that is, they possess a power of compulsion as irresistible as despotic power, they are not sustained by us, they are what sustains us; they therefore dispense with any form of agreement (ARENDT, 1990, p.157).

It's worth pointing out that it was always important that natural law itself needed divine sanction to become binding on men, and that religious sanction began to require more than the theoretical elaboration of a "higher law". For Jefferson, men's opinions and beliefs do not depend on their own will, but involuntarily follow the evidence in their minds.

4.2 Robespierre's approach

According to Arendt, the founding fathers saw themselves as masters of political science. In the 18th century, they collected constitutions - as others collect stamps. They were called *men of letters, which* corresponds to today's intellectuals. Freed from the burden of poverty, they turned to the study of Greek authors - and this was decisive because of their eternal wisdom or immortal beauty. Thus, their main aim was to learn about political institutions in order to bear witness, but freedom for them was public freedom (ARENDT, 1990, p.96).

Robespierre made his preferential choice for the poorest, but this remains debatable. For we cannot ignore the fact that the masses are used by unscrupulous politicians with diverse interests. For Arendt, acts of violence, however perverse, are a sign of intelligence for the masses, and this ultimately attracts the "roundup" towards violent acts. This is confirmed by the altruism of totalitarianism and the success of this form of political regime. Arendt (1951) asserts that: It would be an even greater mistake to forget, in the face of such impermanence, that totalitarian regimes, as long as they are in power, and totalitarian leaders, as long as they are alive, "always command the support of the masses and rely on it" (ARENDT, p.356).

Political actions can influence the masses towards violent action, so that the lack of security affects the opposition government. In contemporary times, we realize that there is a veiled incitement to violence when the media determine that it is relevant to accentuate violent acts committed by human beings. For example, violent acts are shared on social networks with great ease. And it seems that after committing the act, the violent agent records and publishes it on social media, as if to prove that he or she is the "right one" in the act of committing atrocities. However, what is worrying and saddening is that there is a mass of people who share it, thus distorting the vision of something that could not and should not be seen by a human being as something natural.

Robespierre's theory of revolutionary dictatorship, although inspired by the experiences of the revolution, found its legitimization in the famous Roman Republican institute. It should be noted that Robespierre studied at a Christian school until the age of 23, which may have contributed to his choice. He states that constitutional government deals with civil liberty and revolutionary government with public liberty, and that the "principles of revolutionary government" would be to protect and preserve the republic. He adds: "In constitutional government, it is sufficient to protect individuals against the abuses of public power". This shows that power is always public and in the hands of government (ARENDT, 1990, p.97).

The assimilation of power with violence, politics with government and government with necessary evil that has begun is fatal. Fear and hope mingle when we realize that the revolutionary notions of public happiness and public liberty have never disappeared from the American political scene, and have become part of the very structure of the republic's body politic. Arendt argues in her analysis that the exhaustion of the political system's legitimacy is the result of the disintegration of spaces once founded on citizen opinion and action (ARENDT, 1990, p.146).

Secularization, the separation of state and church, left French and American revolutionaries searching for a new absolute. The constituent power needed a new authority. The new droit du sol needed an absolute, and Robespierre desperately sought one when it was no longer attributed to God (ARENDT, 1990, p.148).

From then on, the powerlessness of the individual is realized when he is protected by the government. There has been a flattening of freedom and power, not in the public sphere, but in the private life of the citizen. Arendt reports that the physiognomy of the 19th century, which continued into the 20th, was the conversion of the citizen into a private individual (ARENDT, 1990, p.110).

Absolutism preceded all revolutions, with the exception of the American Revolution. That's why it was necessary to establish a new law for the nation. This law would be, for future generations, the "higher law", which confers validity on all human laws. The idea of a "higher law" underlined the need for an absolute, both in France and in America. And Robespierre was the first to make a clear and unequivocal distinction between the origin of power, which comes from below, from the "deep roots" of the people, and the source of law, which lies "above", in a higher, transcendent region. In the French Revolution, the absolute monarchy's claim to be founded on "divine rights" had given rise to the conception of a god whose will is the law. Whereas in the American Revolution, it was the general will that prevailed (ARENDT, 1990, p.148).

For Hannah Arendt, Robespierre's desperate search for a way to legitimize laws in the absolute ended up overturning the old system. The notion of the "immortal soul", which enabled justice to continue to play its role, became indispensable because it prevented the new sovereign, the absolute monarch, from committing criminal acts. Arendt (1990) puts it this way:

They were all deists, and their insistence on belief in future states was strangely at odds with their religious convictions. It was certainly not any religious fervor, but strictly political apprehensions about the enormous risks inherent in the secular sphere of human relations that prompted them to use the one element of religious tradition whose political utility, as an instrument of government, was beyond doubt (p.153).

For Arendt, the political crime that could be observed on an unprecedented scale, by people who had freed themselves from any belief in "future states" and had lost the age-old fear of an "avenging God", does not allow us to doubt the political wisdom of the founders. But it was political wisdom, not religious conviction, that led them to disrespect mankind (ARENDT, 1990, p.153).

Sanction granted by the Church in the West for many centuries, in which secular laws were understood as a worldly expression of a divinely ordained law (152). Christ's emissaries became authorities, until Protestant rebels rebelled, for natural law, for Jewish laws and covenants and even for the figure of Christ himself, prevailed. As for Robespierre, Arendt (1990) states: "As far as the French Revolution was concerned, he needed a perpetual and transcendent source of authority, which could not be identified with the general will either of the nation or of the revolution itself" (p. 148). The author (1990) states:

This eternity is the absolute of temporality, and insofar as the principle of the universe proceeds from this region of the absolute, it is no longer arbitrary, for it is anchored in something which, though beyond human comprehension, has a reason, a rationality of its own. The curious fact that the men of the revolutions threw themselves into the desperate search for the absolute, at the very moment when they were compelled to act, may well have been influenced, at least in part, by the ancient conceptions and customs of Western civilization, according to which every entirely new principle requires an absolute to serve as its source and by which it is "explained" (p.165).

It is very important here to emphasize how paradoxical it seemed to Arendt that, at the very moment when, historically, the men of the revolutions were dealing with a completely new form of relationship to the spirit of the laws, because they were detaching themselves from the influences of the Churches, and in the 17th century were regarded as the "enlightened", they were seeking to emancipate themselves from this age-old relationship, a kind of religious sanctuary (ARENDT, 1990, 149).

Hannah Arendt argues that what Robespierre achieved with his concept of the

"Supreme Being", which she claims was not even his own expression, was to demonstrate purely and simply the irrelevance of religious beliefs in the political sphere. For the author, there are countless ways of interpreting the problem of the absolute and its configuration in history (ARENDT, 1990, p.148).

In short, Arendt takes the problem of the absolute in terms of the legitimization of politics, something Robespierre tried to achieve with extreme conviction, not religious, but political, even if he desperately resorted to omnipotence. The author asserts in his works that action depends on the will of men who, through their common action, are able to inspire and guide each other's action. A new absolute - omnipotence - prevents human plurality.

4.3 Montesquieu's solution

To present Montesquieu's vision of authority and legitimacy, we need to turn to his reading of political structure in the West. Charles Louis de Secondat - surname - Montesquieu was born in France on January 18, 1689. He was a jurist, historian, philosopher and politician. [1]Montesquieu's most important work was published in 1748 under the title: L'esprit des lois (The Spirit of Laws), when the author was fifty-nine years old, is therefore the product of thought developed in the first half of the 18th century, the work of a thinker, unique in his time, who considered political problems in themselves, without preconceived ideas about mind and nature. Even before the outbreak of the Revolution, Montesquieu was aware that decadence was gradually undermining the foundations of Western political structures. Laws, and the authority of those who govern them, were losing credibility and trust. He feared that freedom would disappear within the framework in which it had taken refuge (ARENDT, 1990, p. 94).

For Arendt, Montesquieu was the first to predict that governments would be easily overthrown and that the gradual loss of authority of all inherited political structures, which he had in mind, would become evident to an increasing number of

---

[1]   *L'Esprit des lois* was published in 1748. The fruit of the Enlightenment, which proclaimed the right of reason, L'Esprit des lois is a work of reference.
Montesquieu's work inaugurates a new perspective in the approach to social and political problems: the exclusion of religious or moral concepts, the abandonment of abstract and deductive theories. His concern was to go beyond the positions of philosophers and utopians who presented their theories in the abstract, without taking into account spatial and temporal determinants (MONTESQUIEU, 1748).

people during the 18th century. [2]According to the author, the collapse of the ancient Roman trinity would play a fundamental role in this decline and fall of political authority (ARENDT, 1990, p.94).

An intriguing new problem has appeared on the scene: secularization. Christianity, which had hitherto dominated minds and hearts with its Roman power, rules and norms, was imposing its own ways of managing political, social and religious life. What would the establishment of a new authority look like without the domination of the Roman Empire? What would the new absolute be: a monarch, as in the French Revolution, or would it be more interesting to base power on the people, as in the American Revolution? According to Arendt, the problem of the absolute is inherent in the revolutionary event itself. Yet the American revolutionaries offered us the chance of perception, far from the historical conviction of what happened in the various revolutions where the authority of the monarch made people believe in its necessity (ARENDT, 1990, p. 156). The author states:[3] Revolutions are the consequence and never the cause of the decadence of political authority (1990, p. 93). The durability of obsolete governments, strange as it may seem, is a fact in the history of Western politics, even in the absence of authority, for men would have to be willing to organize and act together, otherwise disintegration would be inevitable.

According to Arendt, revolutions, and even the American Revolution, were unable to secure the institution of political liberty originating in ancient Greece, and ended up creating a new form of "constitutional" government, resulting in a dose of civil rights in the form of a monarchy or republic, which ultimately merited only the appellation of limited government. For the author, Constitutions, contrary to popular belief, are not the result of revolutions. In a way, they were imposed after the failure of revolutions, which was perceived as a sign of defeat rather than victory (ARENDT, 1990, p. 117).

For Arendt, France and America needed constituent assemblies and special conventions, whose sole task was to draft a constitution. It was permissible to take the draft home and, back to the people, discuss it point by point. If the articles of the Constitution were debated in state conventions, it would be popular participation that

---

[2] Secularization, i.e. the separation of State and Church: Religion - Tradition and Authority.

[3] - Authority, for Hannah Arendt, derives from the Latin verb *augere* (*to* increase), and what political action does in the public space of speech and action is to add, through deeds and events, importance to the foundation of the political community and life to its institutions. The importance of common action and foundation, as the basis of authority (ARENDT, On the Dignity of Politics, pp. 91-141).

would give the government a Constitution in which the people constituted their own government, not the other way around (ARENDT, 1990, p. 116).

Another fundamental element, which the revolutionaries failed to grasp, was the importance of founding a republic, on the one hand, and the fact that the real content of the Constitution was not absolutely the safeguarding of civil rights, but the establishment of an entirely new system of authority, on the other. What the regional charters and the loyal attachment of the colonies to the King and Parliament of England did for the people of America was to give them additional power and weight of authority. This colonial body politic of the New World became the foundation, not of power, but of authority (ARENDT, 1990, p. 118).

For Hannah Arendt (1990): "Power and authority differ as much as power and violence" (p. 118). The author points out that the monumental theme of Montesquieu's work was in fact the constitution of political liberty. But in this context, the word *constitution* has lost all negative connotations, of limiting or negating power. The word now means that "the great temple of federal liberty" must focus on the foundation and proper distribution of power. In this sense, *power and freedom* became linked, along with the *power of* representation (ARENDT, 1990, p. 120). It was impossible to believe that revolutionary power would still resist and remain intact in the face of the uncontrolled consolidation of the way in which the nature of power came to be exercised in political matters. Arendt (1990) states:

Power can only be contained, while remaining intact, by power, so that the principle of the separation of powers not only provides a guarantee against the monopolization of power by one part of government, but also offers a kind of mechanism, built into the very heart of government, by which new power is constantly generated, without, however, developing and expanding to the detriment of other centers or sources of power (p. 121).

For Hannah Arendt, the American Revolution sets an unforgettable example and teaches us an unprecedented bond, for this Revolution did not simply break out, but was led by men who resolved together, united in deed and word by the force of mutual commitments. The author calls the "lost treasure" of the American Revolution the neglect of popular participation and the revolutionary spirit that culminated in American Independence. All political affairs are and always have been dealt with within a framework of lakes and obligations for the future, such as laws and constitutions, treaties and alliances, all of which derive, in the final analysis, from the ability to promote and maintain promise in the face of the intrinsic uncertainties of the future (ARENDT, 1990, p. 212).

The fact is that, precisely because it depended on a tradition dating back to the dawn of Roman history, political authority was the last of the three elements to disappear, namely religion, tradition and authority (ARENDT, 1990, p. 94). Montesquieu, in his political wisdom, was the only one of the founding fathers to support the thesis that power and freedom were linked to each other (ARENDT, 1990, p.120).

Political freedom limited by the moderation of power is a demand that Montesquieu does not renounce. For him, democratic and aristocratic systems are essentially free only if power is not abused. Of virtue itself, he ironizes: "Virtue itself needs limits". The man who has power is most often tempted to abuse it. In everyday practice, we often see people who, when exercising the power they have in their hands, use it in a way that is incompatible with its intended purpose, which is to serve their subordinates. Even if we know that this way of managing power and authority is human, we have no right to follow this model, for it brings more disaffection than peace to human life. Montesquieu persistently searched for the concept of liberty until he arrived at this concept in the political sense (MONTESQUIEU, 1748, p. 334). He thus asserts: "It is better to say that the government most in conformity with nature is that whose particular disposition best relates to the dispositions of the people for whom it was established" (p. 28). Of religions in general, Montesquieu (1748) says:

Just as we can judge among the darkness those that are less thick, and among the abysses those that are less deep, so we can search among the false religions those that are more in keeping with the good of society; those that, although they do not have the effect of producing men for the joys of the hereafter, can contribute more to their happiness in it (p.365).

Montesquieu (1748) set out to examine religions in general, with the aim of realizing the good they can bring to the civil state, both those with roots on Earth and those with roots in Heaven. Of Christianity in particular, he says: "The Christian religion, which commands men to love one another, undoubtedly wants every people to have the best political laws and the best civil laws, because they are, after it, the greatest good that men can give and receive" (p. 365).

For Arendt, Montesquieu is the only one of the proto-revolutionaries not to have considered it necessary to introduce absolute, divine or despotic power into the political sphere. The striking fact is that Montesquieu used the word "loi" in its old Roman sense in his book "L'esprit des lois" to mean the subsisting relationship between different entities. Roman laws were merely the means of establishing peace; they were treaties and agreements with which a new covenant was formed. A curious fact, according to Arendt, is that for the Romans the end of war was not only characterized by the defeat of the enemy, but by the establishment of peace, and the Romans' greatest satisfaction was that their enemies became friends and allies of Rome. The Romans' greatest satisfaction was that their enemies should become friends and allies of Rome, so that the Roman system of alliances could be extended to every country on the planet. (ARENDT, 1990) The author thus asserts:

It is true that he also assumes the existence of a "Creator" and a "Maintainer" of the universe, and that he also speaks of a "state of Nature", and of "natural laws", but the *relationships* that subsist between Creator and creation, or between men in the state of Nature, are merely "rules" or *regions* that define the government of the world, and without which the world would not exist. (p. 151).

According to Arendt, for Montesquieu, neither religious nor natural laws constitute a "higher law" in the strict sense; they are nothing more than existing relationships in which the different states of being are preserved. If, for the Roman, law is purely and simply that which connects two things, and is therefore relative by definition, he needed no source of absolute authority, and could describe the "spirit of laws" without ever raising the problematic question of their absolute validity (ARENDT, 1990, p. 151).

According to Montesquieu, law is what connects, i.e. religious law is what connects man to God. Without divine law, there would be no way to relate to God. And human law is what links men to their fellow men. In Arendtian terms, for Montesquieu, it would be perfectly possible to abuse power while remaining within the bounds of the law, and the need for limitation derives from the nature of human power, not from the antagonism between law and power (ARENDT, 1990, p. 237).

[4]Montesquieu's most famous work, the first chapter of which deals with the relationship between laws and other beings, underlines his conviction that laws, in their broadest sense, are necessary relationships that flow from the nature of all things. Consequently, all beings have their laws, men, animals and divinities have their laws. "Laws, in their broadest sense, are necessary relationships that flow from the nature of things" (p.25).

In short, for Montesquieu, the political life of a country is not determined by any fatality, since men are free and "as intelligent beings, they ceaselessly violate the laws

---

[4] MONTESQUIEU- L'ESPRIT DES LOIS, 1748.

that God has established, modifying also those that they themselves have created". In this sense, the relationships established between the different types of laws in a society are neither inexorable nor independent of human will. Montesquieu tirelessly sought to discover models of society that could inspire legislators. But these same models, which have developed over time, can be analyzed by means of historical induction, as well as deduction that highlights the naturalness and appropriateness of these relationships.

FINAL CONSIDERATIONS :

This text deals with freedom and politics from Hannah Arendt's perspective. As we have seen, Arendt's conceptions of freedom in the realm of politics are very striking.

In *Da Revolución* (1990), the author attempts to evaluate the American Revolution, which leads us to reflect on how, at this moment in history, freedom in politics can be demonstrated. This means that Arendt has linked the ideal of freedom to what was experienced in the United States. On the other hand, Arendt describes the action experienced by the men of the revolution in America as a "lost treasure" in the context of the American revolution. In this context, the public sphere was diluted and suffocated by democracy itself, and freedom came to be confused with the conquest of liberation, which Arendt deems regrettable.

According to Arendt, Thomas Jefferson clearly realized the inevitable failure of the American scenario. His attempts to maintain districts and prevent the dissolution of public space were in vain. And the adoption of representative government became the new form of democracy. Thus, the districts became the instrument by which the wishes of the people were transmitted to their "representatives".

In modern times, democracy has produced a new form of freedom. And the Constitution established the fundamental rules and principles of the political system, formalizing and integrating it into a coherent legal order, in a reversal where the power of a Constitution established in the American Revolution by the people in the public sphere, became in the Republic a government of laws, as the source of authority for the establishment of government.

Authority and legitimacy in Hannah Arendt's conception led to the search for a new absolute after the dissolution of the Roman trinity (religion, tradition, authority). That's why political authority, of these three elements, should be the last to disappear. Based on this author, we set out to assess the implications of the loss of religious sanction for the nature of the absolute. We analyze the following founding fathers - Thomas Jefferson, Robespierre and Montesquieu - and the way they sought to legitimize authority on the political terrain through the question of the absolute.

After the separation of State and Church, the Catholic Church gradually lost its political aspirations, but some of the founding fathers of the American Revolution persisted in their quest for the absolute.

For Hannah Arendt, when we find in Thomas Jefferson and Robespierre a relentless search for a new absolute, the paradox becomes obvious. At the very moment when it was hoped that the "enlightened" men of the 18th century would, in theory and practice, definitively disengage themselves from all forms of religious sanction, the crisis and the emergence of revolutions led to the emergence of a feeling of powerlessness and insecurity. In fact, the crisis and the emergence of revolutions led them to seek a new absolute at the same time as they detached themselves from the influence of the Church in the secular sphere, separating politics from religion. The text developed here deals with authority and legitimacy in Hannah Arendt's conception. As we have seen in the course of this work, her main theme was the search for a new absolute after the dissolution of the Roman trinity (religion, tradition, authority). And why political authority, of these three elements, would be the last to disappear.

Starting with Arendt, we sought to assess the implications of the loss of religious sanction for the nature of the absolute. We analyzed the following founding fathers - Thomas Jefferson, Robespierre and Montesquieu - and the way they sought to legitimize their authority on the political terrain through the question of the absolute. After the separation of State and Church, the Catholic Church gradually lost its political aspiration, but some of the founding fathers of the American Revolution persisted in their quest for the absolute.

For Hannah Arendt, when we find in Thomas Jefferson and Robespierre a relentless search for a new absolute, the paradox becomes obvious. At the very moment when it was hoped that the "enlightened" men of the 18th century would, in theory and practice, definitively disengage themselves from all forms of religious sanction, the crisis and the emergence of revolutions led to the emergence of a feeling of powerlessness and insecurity. In fact, the crisis and the emergence of revolutions led them to seek a new absolute at the same time as they detached themselves from the Church's influence in the secular sphere by separating politics from religion.

Finally, the solution found by Montesquieu, according to Arendt, is the fact that for him Law is everything that connects, i.e. religious law is what connects man to God. In other words, religious law is what links man to God. Indeed, without divine law, there would be no way to connect with God. And human law is what connects people to each other. Laws, in their broadest sense, are necessary relationships that flow from the nature of things, and in this sense, all beings have their laws; divinity has its laws; the material world has its laws; intelligences higher than man have their laws; man has his laws. In Arendtine's terms, for Montesquieu, it would be perfectly possible to abuse power while remaining within the bounds of the laws, and the need for limitation derives from the nature of human power, not from the antagonism between *law* and *power*.

REFERENCES

ARENDT, Hannah. *The Origins of Totalitarianism.* Sao Paulo: Companhia das Letras, 1951.

. *The human condition.* 13. ed. Rio de Janeiro: Forense Universitaria, 1987.

. *Between past and future.* Sao Paulo: Perspectiva, 2000.

. *Da Revolugao.* 2. ed. Rio de Janeiro: Atica; Brasilia Ed. da UnB, 1990.

. *The dignity of politics* - Relume-Dumara, 2002.

BIGNOTTO, Newton. The conflict of liberties: Saint Augustine. *Revista Sintese,* Belo Horizonte, v. 19, n. 58, 1992.

BRITO, Fausto. The rupture of human rights in Hannah Arendt's political philosophy. *Kriterion - Revista de Filosofia,* v. 54, n. 127, p. 7, 2013.

CORREIA, Adriano. *Between the past and the future.* Juiz de Fora: Ed. da UFJF, 2008.

DUARTE, André. Thinking and acting in times of darkness. *Cult Magazine,* Rio de Janeiro, 2010.

ECCEL, Daiane. Hannah Arendt's Socrates: Arendtian Considerations on Socrates. *Inquietude,* Goiania, v. 2, n. 1, p. 62-63, Jan/Jul. 2011.

GALEFFI, Dante Augusto. What is Husserl's phenomenology? *Idiagao,* Feira de Santana, January/June 2000.

HOBSBAWN, Eric J. *The French Revolution.* 5th edition, Paz e Terra, 1996.

HUSSERL, Edmund. *Philosophy as the science of rigor.*
Translated by Albin Biau. Atlantide, 1965.

LAFER, Celso. *The human condition.* Translated by Roberto Raposo. Rio de Janeiro: Forense Universitaria, 1987.

LEON, Facundo Ponce de. *Autoridady Poder.* Montevideo; Taurus, 2014.

MALONE, Dumas. *Thomas Jefferson: a brief biography.* Jefferson and his times. 1993.

MONTESQUIEU, The Spirit of Laws. Sao Paulo: Abril Cultural, 1748.

SCHIO, Sonia Maria. *History and freedom: from action to reflection.* Porto Alegre: Clarinete, 2012.

SOUZA, Vinicius Silva. Hannah Arendt's concept of freedom. Between past and future. Juiz de Fora: Ed. da UFJF, 2008.